GUIDE TO CHICAGO MANUAL OF STYLE

Full Guide to Step-by-Step Formatting for Students

GUIDE TO CHICAGO MANUAL OF STYLE: Full Guide to Step-by-Step Formatting for Students
Student Guide Series, Book 10, Ed. 1

By CreativeCloud Publications
2020

Learn how to format your academic paper in the Chicago Style

This guide focuses on the Chicago Manual of Style (CMOS) footnote/endnote citation system.

The following guide contains the most common areas of CMOS formatting, providing an overview of CMOS and is a great place to start learning about CMOS format.

The guidance is organized to provide you with the reference format for the main type of source material you may need to reference. Most sections also provide a range of examples on how your writing should be formatted:

1. The 1st part of this guide introduces Chicago referencing style.
2. The 2nd part of the guide shows the most common guidelines to format your academic paper.
3. The 3rd part of the guide shows how to cite sources in the main body of your paper and compile the bibliography list at the end of your paper.
4. The 4th part of the guide shows the examples of sources formatting within the paper.
5. The 5th part suggests essential steps on successful formatting for students.
6. The 6th part of the guide contains the paper layout example formatted in the Chicago referencing style.

This guide is intended to help you understand how to use source material effectively in this format. It outlines the general features of the Chicago Manual of Style, but it is important that you follow your department's specific guidelines as there might be some different interpretations and requirements that might be specifically required within your discipline.

This guide is based on The Chicago Manual of Style, Chicago: University of Chicago Press, 17th ed., 2017. Many of the examples and quoted text in this guide are taken from Chapter 14 of CMOS.

The instructor for your class is the final authority on how to format your references.

CreativeCloud Publications
2020

TABLE OF CONTENTS

PART I: INTRODUCTION

1.1 The Chicago Manual of Style (CMOS)

The Chicago Manual of Style (CMOS) is most commonly used by those working in literature, history, and the arts. First published in 1906, the Chicago Manual of Style is the authoritative guide to the Chicago referencing style. The current guide is based on the 17th edition (2017).

The Chicago Manual of Style (CMOS) is primarily intended as a style guide for published works and class papers.

The Chicago Manual of Style (CMOS) includes two systems for citation:
1. an Author-Date (AD) system, which uses parenthetical citations within the text itself, and
2. a Notes and Bibliography (NB) system, which uses footnotes.

These two systems are nearly identical in content, but are different in form.

This guide demonstrates citations in the Notes and Bibliography (NB) system.

1.2 Author-Date (AD) System

As its name suggests, Author-Date (AD) system uses parenthetical citations in the text to reference the source's author's last name and the year of publication. Each parenthetical citation corresponds to an entry on a references page that concludes the document. In these regards, Author-Date (AD) system is very similar to APA style.

1.3 Notes and Bibliography (NB) System

By contrast, Notes and Bibliography (NB) system uses numbered footnotes in the text to direct the reader to a shortened citation at the bottom of the page. This corresponds to a fuller citation on a Bibliography page that concludes the document. Though the general principles of citation are the same here, the citations themselves are formatted differently from the way they appear in Author-Date (AD) system.

History places great emphasis on source origins, so footnotes and endnotes are used to demonstrate on-page where a particular piece of information comes from. In the Notes and Bibliography (NB) system, a number is assigned to a particular fact in the text, and the correlating footnote or endnote will link the source to the text and to the bibliography.

1.4 CMOS Usage

CMOS describes rules for writers and students of:
- History
- English
- Art

CMOS establishes written standards of communication concerning:
- formatting and page layout,
- stylistic techniques,
- citing sources,
- preparing a manuscript for publication.

Abiding by CMOS's standards will allow you to:
- provide readers with cues they can use to follow your ideas more efficiently and to locate information of interest,
- allow readers to focus more on your ideas by eliminating unfamiliar formatting,
- establish your credibility in the field by demonstrating an awareness of your audience and their needs as researchers.

2.1 Paper Format

There are two parts to referencing:
1. the citations within the text of your paper and
2. the reference list at the end of your paper.

- Chicago papers should be double-spaced.
- Footnotes/Endnotes and Bibliography list should be single-spaced, but should have a blank line between entries.
- Set margins of at least 1 inch from the edge of the page on all sides:
  - Margins should be set at no less than 1" and no greater than 1.5".
- Use readable fonts, such as Times New Roman or Courier.
- Font size should be no less than 10 pt (preferably, 12 pt).

2.2 Title Page

Class papers will either include a title page or include the title on the first page of the text. Use the following guidelines if your context requires a title page:

- The title page should take up the full first page of your paper.
- The title should be centered a third of the way down the page.
- Your name and class information should follow several lines later.
- When subtitles apply, end the title with a colon and place the subtitle on the line below the title.
- Double-space each line of the title page.

Example:

MOVING "NETWORKS" INTO THE COMPOSITION CLASSROOM

Jessica Clements
English 626: Postmodernism, Rhetoric, Composition
March 7, 2010

2.3 Header

- The page header should contain the author's last name followed by the page number.
- The first page to be numbered should be the second page (if there is a title page in the work):
  - Don't put a page number on the title page.
  - Begin in the header of the first page of text.
  - Every page except the title page should contain a header.
- A header should be found on the top of page justified to the right.
- In papers that include front matter numbered with roman numerals (such as a dedication or table of contents), the title page counts as page i.

2.4 Headings

While The Chicago Manual of Style does not include a prescribed system for formatting headings and subheads, it makes several recommendations:

- Use headline-style for purposes of capitalization.
- Subheadings should begin on a new line.
- Subheadings can be distinguished by font-size.
- Ensure that each level of hierarchy is clear and consistent.
- Levels of subheads can be differentiated by type style, use of boldface or italics, and placement on the page, usually either centered or flush left.
- Use no more than 3 levels of hierarchy.
- Avoid ending subheadings with periods.
- Subheadings should be used for longer papers.
  - CMOS recommends you devise your own format but use consistency as your guide.

Turabian has an optional system of 5 heading levels, shown below:

1st Level Heading

CENTERED, BOLD, UPPERCASE

2nd Level Heading

CENTERED, REGULAR, UPPERCASE

3rd Level Heading

Flush Left, Bold, Uppercase

4th Level Heading

Flush left, regular, lowercase

5th Level Heading

Intended, bold, lowercase with a period. Run in at beginning of paragraph (no blank line after).

Example in paper layout:

First Level
Lorem ipsum dolor sit amet, porro ullum ne sea, ad vis odio decore. Ne corrumpit gubergren referrentur nec, sed cu quot causae sententiae. Quodsi eleifend pri ut.
Second Level
Lorem ipsum dolor sit amet, porro ullum ne sea, ad vis odio decore. Ne corrumpit gubergren referrentur nec, sed cu quot causae sententiae.
Third Level
Lorem ipsum dolor sit amet, porro ullum ne sea, ad vis odio decore. Ne corrumpit iracundia pri. Euismod hendrerit repudiandae nec at.
Fourth level
Lorem ipsum dolor sit amet, porro ullum ne sea, ad vis odio decore. Ne lobortis iracundia pri. Euismod hendrerit repudiandae nec at.

Fifth level. Lorem ipsum dolor sit amet, porro ullum ne sea, ad vis odio decore. Ne lobortis iracundia pri. Euismod hendrerit repudiandae nec at.

2.5 Main Body

- Text should be double-spaced.
- Block quotations (extracts), notes, bibliography entries, table titles, and figure captions should be single-spaced.
- Chicago takes minimalist approach to capitalization; therefore, while terms used to describe a period are usually lowercased except in the case of proper nouns (e.g., "the colonial period," vs. "the Victorian era").
- Titles mentioned in the text, notes, or bibliography are capitalized "headline-style."
- Titles in the text as well as in notes and bibliographies are treated with quotation marks or italics based on the type of work they name.
    - Book and periodical titles (titles of larger works) should be italicized.
    - Article and chapter titles (titles of shorter works) should be enclosed in double quotation marks.
    - The titles of most poems should be enclosed in double quotation marks, but the titles of very long poems should be italicized.
    - Titles of plays should be italicized.
    - Otherwise, take a minimalist approach to capitalization.
- Italic type can be used for emphasis:
    - Use italics to indicate a foreign word the reader is unlikely to know. If the word is repeated several times (made known to the reader), then it needs to be italicized only upon its first occurrence.

Example:

> …to recognize in all its metamorphoses into the *zones d'attentes* of our airports and certain outskirts of our cities.

- For block quotations (extracts):

- A prose quotation of five or more lines (more than 100 words) should be blocked.
- CMOS recommends blocking two or more lines of poetry.
- A blocked quotation does not need to be enclosed in quotation marks.
- A blocked quotation must always begin with a new line.
- The block quotation should match the surrounding text, and it takes no quotation marks.
- It is also possible to offset the block quotation by using a different or smaller font than the surrounding text.

Example:

> In *Flowers of Freedom: Reframing Political Thought,* Rose eloquently sums up his argument in the following quotation:
>> In a society of control, a politics of conduct is designed into the fabric of existence itself, into the organization of space, time, visibility, circuits of communication. And these enwrap each individual life decision and action—about labour [sic], purchases, debts, credits, lifestyle, sexual contracts and the like—in a web of incitements, rewards, current sanctions and foreboding of future sanctions which serve to enjoin citizens to maintain particular types of control over their conduct. These assemblages which entail the securitization of identity are not unified, but dispersed, not hierarchical but rhizomatic, not totalized but connected in a web or relays and relations. (246)

2.6 Tables and Figures

- Position tables and figures as soon as possible after they are first referenced. If necessary, present them after the paragraph in which they are described.
- For figures, include a caption, or short explanation of the figure or illustration, directly after the figure number.
- Cite the source of the table and figure information with a "credit line" at the bottom of the table or figure and, if applicable, after the caption.
  - Cite a source as you would for parenthetical citation, and include full information in an entry on your Bibliography list.
  - If a table includes data not acquired by the author of the text, include an unnumbered footnote. Introduce the note by the word "source" followed by a colon, then include the full source information, and end the note with a period.
  - Acknowledge reproduced or adapted sources appropriately:
    - photo by…,
    - data adapted from…,
    - map by…, etc.

2.6.1 Citing Figures and Tables

- All figures and tables, referred to in the text or reproduced in an essay, assignment or presentation, must be cited and included in your bibliography list.
- When referring to a figure or table in the text of your essay, give a short citation consisting of the name of the authors, the date of publication or creation and, if appropriate, the relevant page, figure, table, paragraph number or time.

Examples:

Debate raged about the ethics of child care after the publication of the cartoon "Thoughts of a Baby Lying in a Child Care Centre" in the *Sydney Morning Herald* (Leunig 1995, 24).

The power and strength of the female athlete is depicted in Leibovitz's portrait of Jackie Joyner-Kersee (1996, 72).

Ryder has created a framework to illustrate the major factors which influence moral decision making (2006, para. 10).

The fear of the officers, who had no desire to meet with Ned Kelly, is unambiguously portrayed on the face of the trooper in the painting *The Encounter* (Nolan 1946).

- When reproducing an image or a table, a caption should be placed immediately below the image with the appropriate citation.

Examples:

NNN	NNN	NNN	NNN	NNN
NNN	NNN	NNN	NNN	NNN
NNN	NNN	NNN	NNN	NNN

The positive and negative implications of Confucian ideas (Yeh and Xu 2010, table 1).

IMAGE

E-services three-layered structure (Ardagna et al. 2008, fig. 1).

2.7 Standard Abbreviations

Standard abbreviations may be used in your citations.

A list of acceptable, most commonly used abbreviations:

Appendix => app.
Article => art.
Chapter => chap.
Division => div.
Editor, Edited by, Edition => ed.
Editors => eds.
et alii, et aliae (and others) - from Latin => et al.

Manuscript => MS
No date of publication => n.d.
Number(s) => no. (nos.)
No place => n.p.
Page(s) => p. (pp.)
Paragraph => para.
Part => pt.
Revised => rev.
Section => sec.
Series => ser.
sub verso (under the word) - from Latin => s.v.
Supplement => Suppl.
Translator(s) => trans.
Volume => vol.

2.7.1 Place Names

The names of US states and territories are abbreviated in the bibliography list:

- Use the official two-letter U.S. Postal Service abbreviations.

To cite locations outside of the United States, commonly used English names for foreign cities should be used.

The names of Australian states may be abbreviated using standard Australia Post abbreviations.

Examples:

Clevedon, UK: Channel View Publications
French's Forest, NSW: Pearson Australia
Hoboken, NJ: John Wiley & Sons
London: Taylor & Francis
Newbury Park, CA: Sage
Sydney: CCH Australia

Bibliography:

- Create the bibliography page at the end of your paper on a new page. The bibliography should include all sources cited within the work and may sometimes include other relevant sources that were not cited but provided further reading.

Notes (Footnotes/Endnotes):

- Each source have numbered notes with a bibliography entry within the paper. The first note is a full note and the second note is a shortened form that can be used for subsequent citations of a source already cited.

3.2 Bibliography

Bibliographies are typically required by professors for Chicago style papers but are considered optional by the manual itself if full publication information for each source is provided the first time each source is cited in a footnote or endnote. Even though full bibliographic information can be found in the footnotes and endnotes, it is still acceptable, and often required by instructors, to create a bibliography.

The bibliography is placed at the end of an assignment.

Begin the page with the centered heading "Bibliography" and organize entries alphabetically by the last name of each lead author. Notice that source entries on the bibliography page are not formatted exactly the same as footnote/endnote entries:
- punctuation is different and
- the lead author's last name is presented first.

3.2.1 Bibliography Formatting

1. Create the bibliography page at the end of your paper on a new page.
2. Label this page bibliography at the top middle of the page.

The bibliography must also follow this format:

- Centre the word "Bibliography" at the top of a new page.
- Do not underline, bold, enlarge or use quotes for the word Bibliography.
- The bibliography is a list of all the sources used in the paper.
- The list includes the important publication details of the sources.
- Two blank lines should be left between "Bibliography" and your first entry.
- One blank line should be left between remaining entries, which should be listed in letter-by-letter alphabetical order according to the first word in each entry.
- Sources you consulted but did not directly cite may or may not be included (consult your instructor).
- Entries are formatted with hanging indents:

- - the first line is flush with the left margin and all subsequent lines (starting with the second line) are indented.
- List entries in letter-by-letter alphabetical order according to the first word in each entry, be that the author's name or the title of the piece.
- Use "and," not an ampersand, "&," for multi-author entries.
  - For two to three authors, write out all names.
  - For four to ten authors, write out all names in the bibliography but only the first author's name plus "et al." in notes and parenthetical citations.
  - When a source has no identifiable author, cite it by its title.
- Write out publishers' names in full.
- If you cannot ascertain the publication date of a printed work, use the abbreviation "n.d."
- CMOS citation requires the URL or DOI to be listed at the end of the source:
  - Provide DOIs instead of URLs whenever possible.
  - If no DOI is available, provide a URL.
- The date of access should also be included if there is no publication or modification date.
  - Citations for websites should be included in the notes, and only included in the bibliography if there are no notes.
  - Do not use access dates unless publication dates are unavailable.
- If you cannot name a specific page number when called for, you have other options:
  - section (sec.),
  - equation (eq.),
  - volume (vol.), or
  - note (n.).
- The bibliography must be single spaced.

Capitalization

- Capitalize the first and last words in titles and subtitles.
- Capitalize all other major words (nouns, pronouns, verbs, adjectives, adverbs, and some conjunctions).
- English-language book titles and subtitles are capitalized headline-style.

- o In headline style, the first and last words of title and subtitle and all other major words are capitalized.

Abbreviations

ed. or eds. => editor(s)
ed. => edition

Order

- List the sources in alphabetical order by the authors' last names.
- Ignore "A," "And," and "The" when alphabetizing by title if an author is not listed.

Italics or Quotation Marks

- Titles of books, journals and websites are italicized.
- Titles of articles, chapters, webpages, etc. are placed in quotation marks.

Punctuation

- In a bibliography, all major elements are separated by periods.

Spacing

- Entries should be single-spaced, but there should be a blank line between each entry.

General Citing

Generally, Chicago citations require including the following information:
- Author
- Title of book/article
- Title of newspaper/journal
- Publication year
- Publication month and date
- Publisher
- City of publication
- Date of access

- Page numbers
- URL / DOI and Name of Database

3.2.2 Electronic Sources (DOI and URL)

When creating a footnote/endnote or bibliographic entry for an online resource, a DOI and URL are included to help the reader find the source.

DOI

Publishers of peer-reviewed online resources, such as online books and journal articles, usually create a Digital Object Identifier (DOI), which directs the reader to the exact version of the source that the writer originally consulted. A DOI is a permanent ID that, when appended to http://dx.doi.org/ in the address bar of an Internet browser, will lead to the source:
- Include a DOI (Digital Object Identifier) if the publication or book lists one.
- If no DOI is available, list a URL.

URL

- When citing an online source, include a URL, preferably a DOI-based URL (beginning with "https://doi.org/").
- To create a URL from a DOI, append that DOI to "https://doi.org/" to create a URL of the form "https://doi.org/10.1086/679716".

Access Dates

Chicago does not require access dates in its published citations of electronic sources unless no date of publication or revision can be determined from the source.

3.2.3 General Formatting Tips

Authors' Names

- The proper order and spelling of authors' names can be found on the title page of the book or article or on the web page of an internet source.

- If no author is listed, the title of the source becomes the first item of the entry, both for the endnote/footnote and for the bibliography.
- When formatting the bibliography in alphabetical order, items without authors are alphabetized according to the title.

Titles

- The titles of full volumes (books, journals, magazines, newspapers, compact discs, movies, TV shows, podcast series, etc.) are italicized.
- The titles of individual items within those volumes (chapters, articles, songs, scenes, and episodes) are enclosed in quotation marks.

Publisher Names

- Omit words such as "The," "Inc.," and "Co." from publishers' names entirely.
- Do not abbreviate publishers' names.

Publisher Cities

- For well-known cities (London, Toronto, New York), state/province abbreviations and country names are not required.
- Country names are needed for less familiar cities.
- If the name of the state/province is also part of the university press name, the state/province abbreviation is not required.

Page Numbers

- Page number abbreviations "p." or "pp." are typically NOT used in Chicago style.

3.2.4 Authors

One Author

- Last name first, followed by a comma and the first name

Example:

Austen, Jane.

Two to Ten Authors

- The first author's name is inverted:
  - The last name comes first, followed by a comma and the first name.
- All other names are in normal order.

Example:

Stein, George, and Ivan Smith.

More than Ten Authors

- Only the first seven need to be fully cited in the bibliography, the rest of the names can be replaced by the phrase "et al."

Example:

Pitcairn, Dayna L., Diane L. Sabo, Clyde G. Smith, Beverly S. Bernard, D. K. Colborn, Howard E. Rockette, et al.

Multiple Sources by the Same Author

- If you have referred to multiple sources by the exact same author, begin each of the entries with the author's name, as usual.
- The specific order of appearance for that set of sources will then be determined by alphabetical order of the next element of the bibliographical entry, such as the title.

Websites

- Websites need to be listed in the bibliography. For academic papers, most professors expect all sources to be included in the bibliography.

There are some sources that are traditionally left out of bibliographies, such as personal communication (consult your instructor).

3.3 Notes (Footnotes and Endnotes)

3.3.1 General

Most types of citations require two entries:
1. a note and
2. a bibliographic entry.

Notes may be:
- footnotes or
- endnotes.

Notes (footnotes or endnotes) are used to reference pieces of work in the text:
- A superscript number (it is smaller than the normal line of text and raised) is placed after a quote or a paraphrase to cite from a source.
  - Example: Cole found that "The bones were very fragile".[1]
- Each superscript number then refers/corresponds to a numbered citation in the footnotes or endnotes. The matching number in the footnote or endnote is normal sized and not raised:
  - 1. James Smith, *The first and last war*, (New York, Hamilton, 2003), 2.
- A footnote or endnote contains the complete citation information.
- Citation numbers should appear in sequential order:
  - A note number should never appear out of order.
- Footnotes must appear at the bottom of the page that they are referred to.
- Endnotes must appear on an endnotes page:
  - This page should appear immediately before the bibliography page or at the end of the chapter.
- It is up to the discretion of the writer to either place the citation at the bottom of the page where the superscript is placed (footnotes) or to place all citations together at the end of the project (endnotes).

Citation and Note Example:

One would wonder, "Would young Einstein be characterized as belonging somewhere on the autism spectrum? Would Erdos have been given a diagnosis of A.D.H.D.?" [1]

---

1. Silver, Nate. "Beautiful Minds." The New York Times. July 13, 2013. Accessed August 04, 2015. http://www.nytimes.com/2013/07/14/books/review/the-boy-who-loved-math-and-on-a-beam-of-light.html?ref=books&_r=0.

3.3.2 Footnotes

Footnotes appear at the bottom of each page, sometimes separated from the text by an optional short line.

- Note numbers should begin with "1" and follow consecutively throughout a given paper article, or chapter.
- For note numbers in the text, use superscript.
- For note numbers in the notes, use normal text with a period and space after (or use superscript with a space but no period after).
- Each footnote should appear at the bottom of the page that includes its numbered in-text reference.
- The first line of each footnote is indented, typically 0.5" from the left margin (like a paragraph in the main text):
  - Subsequent lines are flush with the left margin.
- Footnotes must be listed in the order in which the superscript numbers appear in the text.
- Each footnote must begin on the same page on which the source is cited, though a long footnote may carry over to the following page.
- Footnotes are single-spaced with one extra space/blank line between notes.
- Footnotes may include commentary and explanation.
- Use a short line to separate footnotes from the main text.
- Use regular text or smaller for the notes.

In the Text:

- Note numbers should be placed at the end of the clause or sentence to which they refer.
- Note numbers should be placed after all punctuation, except for the dash.

In the Footnotes:

- Note numbers are full-sized, not raised, and followed by a period.
- Superscripting note numbers without a period in the notes themselves is also acceptable.
- Place commentary after source documentation when a footnote contains both.

- Separate commentary and documentation by a period:
  - In parenthetical citation, separate documentation from brief commentary with a semicolon.
  - Do not repeat the hundreds digit in a page range if it does not change from the beginning to the end of the range.
- First footnote comprises a complete bibliographic "note" citation for a source, which corresponds to a slightly differently formatted bibliography entry.
- Subsequent note citations can and should be shortened, when all sources are cited in full in a bibliography:
  - Use a shortened note (shortened citation) when a previous citation to the source is given in full in a note. A shortened note consists of:
    - the last name of the first one, two, or three authors,
    - the title of the work cited (shortened to "keyword" version of the title in four or fewer words),
    - the page number cited.

3.3.2.1 Citing the Same Source More than Once:

If a source is used more than once in a research project, follow these guidelines:

The first time the in-text reference is cited you must include:

1. Author's first name and last name,
2. The title of the work cited,
3. Place of publication,
4. Publisher name,
5. Year of publications,
6. Referenced pages.

Example:

1. James Smith, *The first and last war*, (New York, Hamilton, 2003), 2.

1. Author's last name,
2. Shortened title (shortened to "keyword" version of the title in four or fewer words),
3. Page referenced number.

This will reduce the bulk of citation information in the paper.

Examples:

> 1. James Smith, *The first and last war*, (New York, Hamilton, 2003), 2.
> 2. ....
> 3. ....
> 4. Smith, *The first*, 220-221.
>   OR
>   Smith, 220-221

> 1. Cohen, Micah, "Rubio is Losing Support Among Republican Voters." FiveThirtyEight. July 09, 2013. Accessed August 04, 2015. http://fivethirtyeight.com/features/rubio-is-losing-support-among-republican-voters/
> 2. ....
> 3. ....
> 4. Cohen, "Rubio Losing Support", 95
>   OR
>   Cohen, 95

- When the same source is used consecutively, instead of typing in the citation information for a third time, use the abbreviation for ibidem: "Ibid."
    - Ibid. stands for the Latin word, ibidem, that means "in the same place."

- o Add the page numbers immediately following.
- o If the same source and same page number is used consecutively, simply write "Ibid."

Examples:

1. Rosnay, Tatiana De. *Sarah's Key*, 24-27.
2. Ibid., 44.
3. Ibid.
4. Ibid., 133-134.
5. Doerr, Anthony. *All the Light We Cannot See*, 397-401.
6. Ibid., 405.
7. Ibid., 745.

Shortened Note Overview

A full citation is necessary only the first time a source is cited in an essay or chapter:
- Subsequent citations can be shortened to save space.
- A shortened note consists of:
  - o the last name of the first one, two, or three authors,
  - o the title of the work cited (shortened to "keyword" version of the title in four or fewer words),
  - o the page number cited.

Example:

1. E.P. Thompson, "The Moral Economy of the English Crowd in the Eighteenth Century," *Past & Present*, no. 50 (1971): 78-79, http://www.jstor.org/stable/650244.
2. Thompson, "Moral Economy," 78-79.
   OR
Thompson, 78-79

Ibid Overview

If you consecutively cite the same source two or more times in a note (complete or shortened), you may use the word "Ibid" instead:
- Ibid. stands for the Latin word, ibidem, that means "in the same place."

- If you are referencing the same source but different page, follow "Ibid" with a comma and the new page number.

Example:

    1. Newton N. Minow and Craig L. LaMay, *Inside the Presidential Debates: Their Improbable Past and Promising Future* (Chicago: University of Chicago Press, 2008), 24-25.

    2. Minow and LaMay, *Presidential Debates*, 24-25.

    3. Ibid.

    4. Ibid, 28-30.

Please note: *The 17th edition of CMOS now discourages the use of the abbreviation "ibid," when directing readers to the preceding footnote. Instead, writers are encouraged to use the shortened form of the citation.*

Cross-Referencing

Aside from "Ibid.," Chicago style offers cross-referencing for multiple notes with repeated content (for longer / discursive / substantive notes).

Example:

    1. Newton N. Minow and Craig L. LaMay, *Inside the Presidential Debates: Their Improbable Past and Promising Future* (Chicago: University of Chicago Press, 2008), 24-25.

    2. See note 1 above.

Discursive Notes

Discursive or "substantive" notes comment upon the text and need not necessarily include citations:
- When a substantive note does include a citation, the citation comes first and is separated from the commentary by a period.

Example:

3. Lisa Ede and Andrea A. Lunsford, "Collaboration and Concepts of Authorship," *PMLA* 116, no. 2 (March 2001): 354-69, http://www.jstor.org/stable/463522. Ede and Lunsford note that we all agree that writing is inherently social, yet we still rely on individualistic praxis; we still ascribe to pedagogies that encourage the independent author producing concrete (original, honest and "truthful") works.

3.3.3 Endnotes

Endnotes follow the same formatting as footnotes:
- Like footnotes, endnotes are arranged by citation number, in the same order in which they appear in the text.
- Instead of appearing at the bottom of each page, however, endnotes are listed at the end of the paper.
- Endnotes may include commentary.

Endnotes must appear on an Endnotes page.
- The page should be titled "Notes" (centered at top).
- This page should appear immediately before the bibliography page.

3.3.4 Adding or Changing Citation

- Ellipses, or three spaced periods (. . .), indicate the omission of words from a quoted passage.
  - Use ellipses carefully as borrowed material should always reflect the meaning of the original source.
- "Sic" is italicized and put in brackets immediately after a word that is misspelled or wrongly used in an original quotation.
  - You should do this only when clarification is necessary.

Example:

> And these enwrap each individual life decision and action — about labour [*sic*], purchases, debts, credits, lifestyle, sexual contracts and the like — in a web of incitements, rewards, current sanctions and foreboding of future sanctions which serve to enjoin citizens to maintain particular types of control over their conduct.

Book (1 Author)

Notes

General Format:

Number. First name Last name, *Title of Book* (City: Publisher, year), page[s] cited [or chapter number, if no page numbers], URL [incorporating DOI when possible].

Example:

1. Peter W. Rose, *Class in Archaic Greece* (Cambridge: Cambridge University Press, 2012), 95.

2. Branden Hookway, *Interface* (Cambridge, MA: MIT Press, 2014), chap. 2, EBSCOhost.

Bibliography

General Format:

Last name, First name. *Title of Book*. City: Publisher, year. URL [incorporating DOI when possible].

Example:

Rose, Peter W. *Class in Archaic Greece*. Cambridge: Cambridge University Press, 2012.

Hookway, Branden. *Interface*. Cambridge, MA: MIT Press, 2014. EBSCOhost. Wang, Xinyuan. Social Media in Industrial China. London: UCL Press, 2016. https://doi-org.uml.idm.oclc.org/10.14324/111.9781910634646.

Book (2-3 Authors / Translated)

Notes

General Format:

Number. First name Last name [first author], First name Last name [second author], and First name Last name [third author], *Title of Book* (City: Publisher, year), page[s] cited.

Example:

1. Massimo Bucciantini, Michele Camerota, and Franco Giudice, *Galileo's Telescope: A European Story,* trans. Catherine Bolton (Cambridge, MA: Harvard University Press, 2015), 8.

Bibliography

General Format:

Last name, First name [first author], First name Last name [second author], and First name Last name [last author]. *Title of Book*. City: Publisher, year.

Example:

Bucciantini, Massimo, Michele Camerota, and Franco Giudice. *Galileo's Telescope: A European Story*. Translated by Catherine Bolton. Cambridge, MA: Harvard University Press, 2015.

Book (4-10 Authors / Edited)

Notes

General Format:

Number. First name Last name [first author], et al., eds. [if edited volume], *Title of Book*, edition. (City: Publisher, year), page[s] cited.

1. Nancy Waxler-Morrison et al., eds., *Cross-Cultural Caring: A Handbook for Professionals,* 2nd ed. (Vancouver: University of British Columbia Press, 2005), 4.

Bibliography

Last name, First name [first author], First name Last name [all authors between first and last], and First name Last name [last author], eds. [if edited volume] *Title of Book*. Edition. City: Publisher, year.

Waxler-Morrison, Nancy, Elizabeth Richardson, Joan Anderson, and Natalie Chambers, eds. *Cross-Cultural Caring: A Handbook for Professionals*. 2nd ed. Vancouver: University of British Columbia Press, 2005.

Chapter in an Edited Book

Notes

Number. First name Last name of chapter author, "Title of Chapter," in *Title of Book*, ed. First name Last name of editor[s], (City: Publisher, year), page[s] cited.

1. James Kirk, "The 'Privy Kirks' and Their Antecedents: The Hidden Face of Scottish Protestantism," in *Voluntary Religion: Papers Read at the 1985 Summer Meeting and the 1986 Winter Meeting of the Ecclesiastical History Society,* ed. W. J. Sheils and Diana Wood (n.p.: Basil Blackwell, 1986), 158.

Bibliography

General Format:

Last name, First name of chapter author. "Title of Chapter." In *Title of Book*, edited by First name Last name of editor[s], chapter/page span. City: Publisher, year.

Example:

Kirk, James. "The 'Privy Kirks' and Their Antecedents: The Hidden Face of Scottish Protestantism." In *Voluntary Religion: Papers Read at the 1985 Summer Meeting and the 1986 Winter Meeting of the Ecclesiastical History Society,* edited by W. J. Sheils and Diana Wood, 155-70. N.p.: Basil Blackwell, 1986.

E-Book

Notes

Example:

1. Association of the Menhaden Oil and Guano Manufacturers of Maine, *The Menhaden Fishery of Maine: With Statistical and Historical Details, Its Relations to Agriculture, and as a Direct Source of Human Food; New Processes, Products, and Discoveries* (Portland: B. Thurston, 1878), 45, https://hdl.handle.net/2027/hvd.32044107318388.

2. Jane Austen, *Pride and Prejudice* (New York: Penguin Classics, 2007), loc. 382 of 1288, Kindle.

3. Philip B. Kurland and Ralph Lerner, eds., *The Founders' Constitution* (Chicago: University of Chicago Press, 1987), chap. 4, doc. 23, para. 4, accessed February 28, 2010, http://press-pubs.uchicago.edu/founders/.

Bibliography

Example:

Association of the Menhaden Oil and Guano Manufacturers of Maine. *The Menhaden Fishery of Maine: With Statistical and Historical Details, Its Relations to Agriculture, and as a Direct Source of Human Food; New Processes, Products, and Discoveries.* Portland: B. Thurston, 1878. https://hdl.handle.net/2027/hvd.32044107318388.

Austen, Jane. *Pride and Prejudice.* New York: Penguin Classics, 2007. Kindle.

Kurland, Philip B., and Ralph Lerner, eds. *The Founders' Constitution.* Chicago: University of Chicago Press, 1987. Accessed February 28, 2010. http://press-pubs.uchicago.edu/founders/.

Journal Article / E-Journal Article

Notes

General Format:

Number. First name Last name, "Title of Article," *Journal* volume, no. issue (year): page[s] cited, URL [when online version is consulted].

Example:

1. Rex Buck Jr. and Wilson Wewa, "'We Are Created from This Land': Washat Leaders Reflect on Place-Based Spiritual Beliefs," *Oregon Historical Quarterly* 115, no. 3 (2014): 303, https://doi-org.uml.idm.oclc.org/10.5403/oregonhistq.115.3.0298;

2. E.P. Thompson, "The Moral Economy of the English Crowd in the Eighteenth Century," *Past and Present,* no. 50 (1971): 78-79, http://www.jstor.org.uml.idm.oclc.org/stable/650244.

Bibliography

General Format:

Last name, First name. "Title of Article." *Journal* volume, no. issue (year): page span. URL [when online version is consulted].

Example:

Buck, Rex, Jr. and Wilson Wewa. "'We Are Created from This Land': Washat Leaders Reflect on Place-Based Spiritual Beliefs." *Oregon Historical Quarterly* 115, no. 3 (2014): 298-323. https://doi-org.uml.idm.oclc.org/10.5403/oregonhistq.115.3.0298.

Thompson, E. P. "The Moral Economy of the English Crowd in the Eighteenth Century." *Past and Present,* no. 50 (1971): 76-136. http://www.jstor.org.uml.idm.oclc.org/stable.

Magazine / Newspaper

Notes

General Format:

Number. First name Last name, "Title of Article," Column Title [if applicable], *Magazine or Newspaper Name* (mobile app [if used]), Month year [or Month day, year], section [if applicable], page[s] cited [if available], URL [when online version is consulted].

Example:

1. Natasha Singer, "Can't Put Down Your Device? That's by Design," *New York Times*, December 6, 2015, sec. BU, 4.

2. Alexandra Schwartz, "Improving Ourselves to Death," *New Yorker*, January 15, 2018, https://www.newyorker.com/magazine/2018/01/15/improving-ourselves-to-death.

3. Paul Bloom, "The War on Reason," *The Atlantic* (iPhone app), March 2014.

Bibliography

Encyclopedia / Dictionary / Lexicon / Concordance

Notes

Bibliography

Encyclopedia and dictionary references are typically not included in CMOS bibliographies.

Multi-Volume Work

Notes

Example:

1. Charles Hodge, *Systematic Theology* (Grand Rapids, MI: Eerdmans, 1946), 2:257.

Bibliography

Example:

Hodge, Charles. *Systematic Theology.* Vol. 2. Grand Rapids, MI: Eerdmans, 1946.

Dissertation or Thesis

Notes

Example:

1. Mark L. Dalbey, "A Biblical, Historical, and Contemporary Look at the   Regulative Principle of Worship" (D.Min. diss., Covenant Theological Seminary, 1999), 92.

Bibliography

Example:

Dalbey, Mark L. "A Biblical, Historical, and Contemporary Look at the Regulative Principle of Worship." D.Min. diss., Covenant Theological Seminary, 1999.

Lecture

Notes

Example:

    1. David Calhoun, "Ancient and Medieval Church History" (lecture, Covenant Theological Seminary, St. Louis, MO, November 14, 2002).

Bibliography

Example:

Calhoun, David. "Ancient and Medieval Church History." Lecture, Covenant Theological Seminary, St. Louis, MO, November 14, 2002.

Website

Notes

General Format:

    Number. First name Last name [if applicable], "Title of Webpage," Website publisher [if indicated], Month day, year [of publication, modification, or access], URL.

Example:

    1. Paul Lynch, Allen Brizee, and Elizabeth Angeli, "Planet X? 9th Planet, beyond Pluto, May Exist, New Study Suggests," Canadian Broadcasting Corporation, last modified January 21, 2016, http://www.cbc.ca/news/technology/9th-planet-x-1.3412070.

    2. "The Canadian Style," Translation Bureau, Public Works and Government Services Canada, accessed April 18, 2018, http://www.btb.termiumplus.gc.ca/tpv2guides/guides/tcdnstyl/index-eng.html?lang=eng

Bibliography

General Format:

Last name, First name [if applicable]. "Title of Webpage." Website
　　publisher [if indicated]. Month day, year [of publication,
　　modification, or access]. URL.

Example:

Associated Press. "Planet X? 9th Planet, beyond Pluto, May Exist,
　　New Study Suggests." Canadian Broadcasting Corporation.
　　Last modified January 21, 2016.
　　http://www.cbc.ca/news/technology/9th-planet-x-1.3412070.

Government of Canada. "The Canadian Style." Translation Bureau,
　　Public Works and Government Services Canada. Accessed
　　April 18, 2018.
　　http://www.btb.termiumplus.gc.ca/tpv2guides/guides/tcdnstyl
　　/index-eng.html?lang=eng

Government Documents

Notes

General Format:

　　　　Number. Issuing Country, Government Division, Named
Subsidiary Divisions, *Document Title,* by First Name Last Name,
Report Number or Name (City: Publisher, year), page[s] cited.

Example:

　　　　1. Government of Canada, Environment Canada, Canadian
Wildlife Service, *How Much Habitat is Enough?* 3rd ed. (Toronto:
Environment Canada, 2013), 25.

Bibliography

General Format:

Issuing Country. Government Division. Named Subsidiary
   Divisions. *Document Title,* by First Name Last Name. Report
   Number or Name. City: Publisher, year.

Example:

Government of Canada. Environment Canada. Canadian Wildlife
   Service. *How Much Habitat is Enough?* 3rd ed. Toronto:
   Environment Canada, 2013.

Film / TV

Notes

General Format:

   Number. First Name Last Name of content author [if critical
commentary or other ancillary content,] *Title of Work,* directed by
First name Last name, (year of studio release; City: Studio, year of
physical copy), format [including URL if online], length [for physical
copy].

Example:

   1. *Smoke Signals,* directed by Chris Eyre (1998; Toronto:
eOne, 2000), DVD, 98 min.

   2. *Dune,* directed by David Lynch (1984;
https://amazon.com/gp/product/B000I9S64U/).

Bibliography

General Format:

Last Name, First Name of director, dir. *Title of Work.* Year of studio
   release. City: Studio, year of physical copy. Format
   [including URL if online], length [for physical copy].

Example:

Eyre, Chris, dir. *Smoke Signals.* 1998. Toronto: eOne, 2000. DVD, 98 min.

Lynch, David, dir. *Dune.* 1984. https://amazon.com/gp/product/B000I9S64U/.

Online Multimedia

Notes

General Format:

Number. First Name Last Name of content author, Title of Work [in italics or quotes], produced by First Name Last Name, Original Publisher, original production /recording date, in production/recording location [if important], Publisher of online edition, online publication date, format/multimedia type, digital file type [if downloaded], length, URL.

Example:

1. Stephen Chew, "How to Get the Most out of Studying," part 1, "Beliefs that Make You Fail . . . or Succeed," 2011, Samford Office of Marketing and Communication, August 16, 2011, video, 6:53, https://youtu.be/RH95h36NChI.

2. "Misty Copeland and Yo Yo Ma," from a performance on *The Late Show with Stephen Colbert* televised by CBS on October 6, 2015, video, 2:05, http://www.globaltv.com/thelateshowwithstephencolbert/video/clips/misty-copeland-and-yo-yo-ma/video.html?v=539164739703.

Bibliography

General Format:

Last Name, First Name of content author. Title of Work [in italics or quotes], produced by First Name Last Name, Original Publisher, original production/ recording date, in production/recording location [if important]. Publisher of online edition, online publication date. Format/multimedia type, digital file type [if downloaded], length. URL.

Example:

Chew, Stephen. "How to Get the Most out of Studying." Part 1, "Beliefs that Make You Fail . . . or Succeed." 2011. Samford Office of Marketing and Communication, August 16, 2011. Video, 6:53. https://youtu.be/RH95h36NChI.

"Misty Copeland and Yo Yo Ma." From a performance on *The Late Show with Stephen Colbert* televised by CBS on October 6, 2015. Video, 2:05. http://www.globaltv.com/thelateshowwithstephencolbert/video/clips/misty-copeland-and-yo-yoma/video.html?v=539164739703.

Step 1: Record

At the time of reading a document, record all of the information necessary to create a citation. The data you record should include the page numbers for direct quotations and for journal articles.

The descriptive elements for a variety of document types are listed below. They will help you to keep the information necessary to create your references.

Books

- Author's surname and name
- Title of publication
- Title of series, if applicable
- Volume number or number of volumes, if applicable
- Edition, if not the first
- Editor, reviser, compiler or translator, if other than the author
- Publisher
- Place of publication (first named)
- Year of publication
- Page numbers, if applicable

Parts of Books

In addition to the details for the Books record the following information specific to the parts of books:
- Author's surname and name (of the part)
- Title of the part
- Inclusive page numbers of the part

Journal Articles

- Author's surname and name
- Title of the article
- Title of the journal
- Volume and issue number
- Year of publication
- Inclusive page numbers

Electronic Documents

For electronic journal articles, record the descriptive elements specified above for journal articles. In addition, record relevant data from the list below.

The following is a list of common descriptive elements you may need to record for citation of an electronic document.

- Authors surname and name
- Title of the document
- Title of the webpage
- Database name
- Page or section numbers if given
- Format (online / cdrom / electronic)
- Year of publication / latest update date
- Internet address
- DOI

Step 2: Organize

- File or store the source documents in a manner and format that is easily accessed at a later date.
- You may wish to write all details on the print copy of an article you are using. Alternatively, you may decide to maintain a master reference list on your computer, which you add details to as required.
- You can also use EndNote to manage your references and produce bibliography list in a specified style.

Step 3: Cite

Construct your citations within the text of your paper, using the appropriate guidelines for the Chicago style.

Step 4: List

Create a bibliography list at the end of your paper:

- Titles of books and journal titles should be italicized.
- The use of capitals and punctuation should be consistent according to Chicago style.

- The usual arrangement for a reference list in Chicago style is a single sequence in alphabetical order by author, with the author's surname preceding the name.
- Where an item has no author, it is usual to list it alphabetically by title in the reference list in sequence by the first significant word of the title.

MOVING "NETWORKS" INTO THE COMPOSITION CLASSROOM

Jessica Clements
English 187: Postmodernism, Rhetoric, Composition
December 28, 2019

In *Democracy and Other Neoliberal Fantasies*, Jodi Dean argues that "imagining a rhizome might be nice, but rhizomes don't describe the underlying structure of real networks,"[1] rejecting the idea that there is such a thing as a nonhierarchical interconnectedness that structures our contemporary world and means of communication.

Michael Hardt and Antonio Negri, on the other hand, argue that the Internet is an exemplar of the rhizome: a non-hierarchical, non-centered network—a democratic network with "an indeterminate and potentially unlimited number of interconnected nodes [that] communicate with no central point of control."[2] What is at stake in settling this dispute?

---

1. Jodi Dean, Democracy and Other Neoliberal Fantasies: Communicative Capitalism and Left Politics (Durham: Duke University Press, 2009), 30.

2. Michael Hardt and Antonio Negri, "Postmodernization, or the Informatization of Production," in *Empire* (Cambridge, MA: Harvard University Press, 2000), 299.

Bibliography

Agamben, Giorgio. *Homo Sacer: Sovereign Power and Bare Life.* Translated by Daniel Heller-Roazen. Stanford: Stanford University Press, 1998.

Dean, Jodi. *Democracy and Other Neoliberal Fantasies: Communicative Capitalism and Left Politics.* Durham: Duke University Press, 2009.

DeLanda, Manuel. *A New Philosophy of Society: Assemblage Theory and Social Complexity.* London: Continuum, 2006.

Ede, Lisa and Andrea A. Lunsford. "Collaboration and Concepts of Authorship." *PMLA* 116, no. 2 (March 2001): 354-69. http://www.jstor.org/stable/463522.

Foucault, Michel. "The Means of Correct Training." In *The Foucault Reader*, 188-205. Edited by Paul Rabinow. New York: Pantheon, 1984.

Rose, Nikolas. "Control." In *Powers of Freedom: Reframing Political Thought,* 233-73. Cambridge: Cambridge University Press, 1999.

Thomas, Nicholas. "Pedagogy and the Work of Michel Foucault." *JAC* 28, no. 1-2 (2008): 151-80.

Toulmin, Stephen. *Cosmopolis: The Hidden Agenda of Modernity.* Chicago: University of Chicago Press, 1990.

Note: *For the purpose of demonstrating a variety of sources, this page contains references that do not match the preceding paper. This is only a sample of how bibliography might be laid out at the end of your paper.*

Please remember: *In a real paper, only the sources you have actually read are referenced in the bibliography.*

SOURCES

For further clarification on the Chicago in-text citation style of footnotes and endnotes, more detailed examples, the CMOS author-date style, or other items consult The Chicago Manual of Style (17th edition), which you can find at your local library or at most major bookstores.

For more information, you may also find it useful to consult Kate L. Turabian's Manual for Writers of Research Papers, Theses, and Dissertations (8th edition), which presents what is commonly known as the "Turabian" citation style.

The CMOS has a website that answers some frequently asked questions and offers extra advice:
- www.chicagomanualofstyle.org

Students may also wish to check the following website for information on Chicago format:
- http://owl.english.purdue.edu

The instructor for your class is the final authority on how to format your references.

Made in the USA
Coppell, TX
28 January 2021